LESSONS OF LIFE
A Survival Manual

By
Lee I. Schwartz

DORRANCE PUBLISHING CO., INC.
PITTSBURGH, PENNSYLVANIA 15222

Copyright © 1993 by Lee I. Schwartz
All Rights Reserved
ISBN # 0-8059-3378-6
Printed in the United States of America

First Printing

TABLE OF CONTENTS

Acknowledgements	ix
Introduction	xi
LESSONS:	
1. The Common Denominator	1
2. Survival	1
3. Loyalty	2
4. Respect	3
5. Self-Respect	4
6. A Can Do Attitude	5
7. Failure	7
8. Balance	8
9. Off Balance	8
10. Life Balance	9
11. Communication	10
12. Actions Speak Louder Than Words	12
13. Performance	13
14. Systems	14
15. Learning, Education, and Practice	15
16. Why?	16
17. Fear and the Unknown	16
18. False Gods	17
19. All We Need Is Love	18
20. In Search of Love (Peer Pressure)	19
21. Environment (A State of Mind)	20
22. The 22 Billion Dollar Move	22
23. Good vs. Evil	24
24. The World Is a Dangerous Place	25
25. Life Roads	26

26. The World Is a Stage	26
27. Risk Reduction	27
28. The Hand Is Quicker Than the Eye	28
29. The Power of Laughter	29
30. Relaxation Is Good for the Mind	30
31. Play the Cards That Are Dealt	31
32. Real Men	32
33. Real Women	32
34. Change	33
35. Time Is Now	33
36. Information, Please	34
37. Tennis, Everyone!	35
38. Great Talent Will Find You; All You Need to Do Is Recognize It	36
39. The End of the Road	38
40. Faith And Miracles	40
41. It's Not Where You Start The Race, It's Where You Finish That Counts	41
42. It Starts With the Customer	42
43. Dealing With Bullies	44
44. Economic Reality	44
45. Sex: A Human Activity	45
46. Hate	46
47. Your Side of the Line	47
48. Hypocrisy	48
49. Make Your Word Your Bond	49
50. Heart	50
51. Less Is More	50
52. Experience vs. Youth	51
53. A Handicap	52
54. Do You Feel Lucky Today?	53

55. When Two Worlds Collide	54
56. The Classless Society	55
57. Imagination and Dreams	56
58. Solve the Problem	57
59. A Little Bit of Knowledge	58
60. The Meaning of the Word *Sale* & Other Economic Concepts	59
61. Stick to the Basics	60
62. Common Knowledge, or Just the Facts, Please	61
63. Go for It!	62
64. Ideas	62
65. The Team	63
66. Window of Opportunity	64
67. One Look Backwards, Two Steps Forward	65
68. Continuation	66
69. Zest for Life	66
70. Ride the Elephant	67
71. Death	67

I would like to acknowledge and express my appreciation to the following individuals for their contribution to the success of this book:

Jeanette Schwartz, Charles Schwartz, Charles H. Schwartz, Debbie LaFauci, Joan Schwartz, Samuel Schwartz, Saddie Schwartz, Rose Spitzer, Leon Spitzer, Sylvia Harris, Dave Harris, Sidney Spitzer, Rae Spitzer, Wally Loeb, Benjamin Serota, Shirley Serota, Betty Pappas, Connie Pappas, Carl Schwartz, and Ethel Schwartz.

INTRODUCTION

At the age of thirty-nine I decided to write a book containing all the lessons I have learned throughout life. These lessons, gained by observation and experience, are my personal philosophy and framework for living. Operating within this framework has brought me great success, joy, spiritual relief, inspiration, and strength.

These lessons, some of which were gained at a great personal cost, are for you to use. It is my hope that each lesson will give you a new or different perspective. Understanding and following the lessons can motivate and challenge you to improve yourself. Please feel free to use this survival manual as a reference guide; as a new or different problem presents itself, read again those lessons that will be most helpful in the situation.

The best to you as you learn the **LESSONS OF LIFE**.

☐ LESSON #1: THE COMMON DENOMINATOR

Every person (there are approximately five billion of us) no matter how special, successful, rich, or poor has three things in common:

- We are BORN
- We DIE
- The time between birth and death marks the character of a person's life. This is SURVIVAL. We are all trying to SURVIVE.

☐ LESSON #2: SURVIVAL

If you are reading this book, event number one has occurred—you were born—and event number two—death—has not occurred. This leaves the middle part, Survival, which is nothing more than the gap between the two.

Blink your eyes—that is how fast a person can die. Cherish each day, each minute, each second, and each encounter with another person as an opportunity because it could be your last.

☐ LESSON #3: LOYALTY

Loyalty means believing in someone when others do not. It is easy to be loyal when times are smooth and things are going right. Yet the real loyalist is the person who is loyal in times of crisis, when things are going wrong. Real loyalists do not jump ship; they support the people they believe in. Loyalty is a two-way street, and it should not be given blindly but should be given to those who give it in return.

Growing up on the streets of Philadelphia as a kid who did not have many material things, I was impressed by loyalty. Loyalty was rare; it was something very special, an asset. Yet unlike other assets, it is one that money cannot buy. I remember growing up in a neighborhood where people looked out for one another. In times of crisis people did not call 911 but counted on the people around them because they were people you could trust. Whether it was taking someone to the hospital in the middle of the night, or baking a cake for a sweet-sixteen party, or providing moral support, the loyalists were always there.

☐ LESSON #4: RESPECT

Respect is a lot like loyalty; to receive it you must first give it.

Uncle Leon was my mother's younger brother; he taught me many valuable lessons. From the age of ten until the age of sixteen I spent many weekends helping him with his work, delivering dry cleaning and working in various pizza restaurants. He was a jovial man with a great sense of humor. I did not come across many people who did not like him. The only times I saw him really angry were those occasions when he did not receive the required respect. I remember visiting him at work and demanding that he drive me home. He became furious with me and said, "Are you asking me or telling me? If you are telling me, get the hell out of here and walk home." He was right; I was telling him. I walked home. The walk home gave me the chance to think about what I did wrong. It also helped me to understand the idea of RESPECT.

Respect is as simple as saying "please" and "thank you." It is calling a person by their title, i.e., doctor, professor, aunt, or uncle. In my family it was disrespectful if you did not use the title of aunt or uncle when addressing the person. Committing such a sin would bring down the wrath of the entire family upon you. Respect is common courtesy and showing good manners. It is playing by a set of rules and understandings. One sure fire way to get on my wrong side is to be disrespectful. Before you can show respect to others, you must respect yourself.

☐ LESSON #5 : SELF-RESPECT

Self-respect is nothing more than believing in yourself. It is realizing that everyone has certain skills, gifts, strengths, and weaknesses. Examine your set of strengths and weaknesses, understand your strengths, and try to improve those skills that are weak. Yet do not become overwhelmed by your weaknesses. It requires a continual process of self-examination, self-improvement, and self-development. Through this process you will gain self-respect and confidence in your abilities that will produce a CAN DO ATTITUDE.

During my first years in high school, I was an average student—not bad but nothing to write home about, either. At the beginning of my senior year in high school I decided to change that. I decided to be the best business student in the entire school (about 300 students). This was quite a bold statement for someone who was only getting B's & C's. Through the above process I gained self-respect and confidence. After the year I found myself on stage in front of the entire school accepting the prestigious Arron Hoffman award for the best business school student of the year! A CAN DO ATTITUDE will produce success.

☐ LESSON #6: A CAN DO ATTITUDE

Nothing succeeds like a CAN DO ATTITUDE. A CAN DO ATTITUDE is a winning attitude. It is looking at half a glass of water as half full, not as half empty. You have to imagine yourself doing before you do. You have to picture yourself winning that award one year before it happens. If you do it, you have a CAN DO ATTITUDE. If you can't do it, then you don't really believe in yourself and, probably, no one else will believe in you, either.

Throughout my life I have met all types of people in all kinds of occupations who have a negative attitude. They are the people who tell you it can't be done. It is too difficult. It is impossible. No, I can't do it. The reasons, explanations, and excuses seem reasonable, true, and correct. When you meet these people or during those rare times when you find yourself in a negative, depressive attitude you MUST fight it. You MUST turn your thinking to CAN DO positive thoughts.

During my early years, some people with negative attitudes would tell me not to dream, not to imagine, and not to try. If enough people tell you that you won't succeed you will probably believe it. Most of us have gone through this negative reinforcement. Because of my early years, I know that negative thoughts will surface in my mind. I also know that I have to fight them and fight the impulse to think negatively even though it is easier to think negative thoughts than to think positively. To think positive thoughts you must consider alternatives and possibilities. This process is time-consuming and difficult. Yet to think negative thoughts you need only to say NO.

In my senior year of high school, after much confusion and wavering I decided to attend Community College of Philadelphia. It was a decision that my mother and other family members supported. Yet my high school counselor, without really knowing me, decided that because I lacked college preparation courses, it would be too difficult for me and I would fail. More than once the counselor tried to convince my mother of this fact. She insisted that my mother have me attend a trade school, for which she thought I was better suited. My mother told her that I made the decision to attend college, that was what I wanted to do, and that was what I would do. Well, the counselor was partially correct; it was difficult for me, especially that first year.

Yet not only did I graduate from Community College with honors, but I went on to earn a Bachelor of Science degree, graduating at the top ten percent of my class. Furthermore, I went on to earn a Master of Business Administration. I found myself teaching business courses at the very same Community College from which I graduated. Not bad for someone whose high school counselor said should learn a trade.

There is nothing more powerful than the human brain. When I was in the U.S. Army I saw people do things that they could never have imagined. They succeeded because of the human brain, A CAN DO ATTITUDE, and an unshakable belief in themselves. That is all it takes to beat the odds.

☐ LESSON #7: FAILURE

You cannot really appreciate success until you have known failure.

It is okay to fail, but don't do it too often. When you do fail, the results of your failure should not be too great. No one succeeds every time; everyone fails at sometime. That is why we have erasers, why baseball hitters get three strikes before they're out, and why football teams get four downs to make ten yards.

Learn from your mistakes and improve your performance. It is all right to make different mistakes, but the person who keeps making the same mistake repeatedly is a fool.

JUST BECAUSE YOU HAVE FAILED DOES NOT MEAN YOU ARE A FAILURE. Separate the one or two failures from the person and remember your successes.

☐ LESSON #8: BALANCE

To be successful your life must be balanced. When baking a cake, if you don't have the right ingredients or the right amount of each ingredient, and if you do not mix the ingredients in the right order, you will not have a very good cake. Balance is getting the right ingredients in the correct proportions and mixing them correctly.

If you eat too much you will gain weight, and if you do not eat enough you will lose weight. Gain enough weight and you become fat; lose enough weight and you will become ill. Work too hard, you will become fatigued; and work too little, you will become lazy. Balance is eating enough without becoming overweight or ill, and it is working hard without becoming worn out.

Nature has a very good life balance. There are four seasons. There is day and night. There is life and death. There is time for all things: a time to work, a time to play, a time to eat, a time to rest.

Find a natural rhythm and balance in your life. Stay centered and don't let people or events move you off balance.

☐ LESSON #9: OFF BALANCE

When you are off balance (Not Centered), you are at your weakest point. You may be too emotional or too angry to take positive actions.

Twenty years of negotiating contracts, through some very heated discussions, taught me to be centered. I remember one such discussion when an armored car carrier requested a ten percent rate increase. I believed that the carrier only needed a five percent increase. A very heated discussion ensued during which the president of that company yelled (shouting names at me that I will not repeat here) and pounded his fists on the table as though they were drumsticks. During all of this I remained cool, calm, and centered. I thanked him for coming and adjourned the meeting. About a week later I received a letter from the armored car carrier's president informing me that he was withdrawing his request for a rate increase. Amazing, staying balanced is POWER!

Staying centered and balanced in such situations is easier said then done; it is like walking a tight rope without a net. Yet to stay centered I will think of another picture in my mind: the ocean, my family, the weather, anything but the conflict. Simultaneously you must be aware of the conflict so you can take the appropriate actions. Also, whatever happens during the conflict, don't take it personally—it is a game and you should treat it as such.

The prime objective of the game is to stay balance while simultaneously trying to weaken your opponent by getting him off balance.

☐ LESSON #10: LIFE BALANCE

A life balance is understanding priorities, keeping the right proportions of those ingredients that make up one's life.

When I see a person who uses drugs, a person who has dropped out of school, or a person who is unkind to others, I seen a person unbalanced in life.

Remember, to gain a life balance you need the right ingredients mixed in the right proportions.

☐ LESSON #11: COMMUNICATION

Achieving effective communication is difficult to do. History is filled with wars that were started over poor communication. How many relationships have ended because of poor communication? How often have you wished for better communication between family members, co-workers, superiors, and friends?

Effective communication is UNDERSTANDING—understanding that occurs between the sender of a message and the receiver of the message. It sounds simple and should be an easy skill to master, but it is NOT easy because of **NOISE**.

Noise is anything that interferes with effective communication (understanding). It could be physical noise, such as an airplane going by a building or loud music playing on the radio. Also, the sender or receiver can create noise. When a sender does not use the appropriate language, does not speak or write clearly, does not use the appropriate sending device, noise occurs. If the receiver does not trust the sender, noise occurs. When the receiver does not actively listen to the sender or prejudges the message, noise occurs. Think about the number of times you have said, But I thought you meant this, and another person responds with, No, I mean this.

Effective communication should be easy because from the time of birth we all communicate with each other. Right? From the time we are born we communicate with our mother and father; then we go through the process of learning language, symbols, writing, reading, and speaking. Still some people do not think of effective communication as a learned skill. Many believe that because they have learned other skills, e.g., reading, writing, and speaking, they can effectively communicate with anyone. Wrong!

If you want to improve your communication, you must think of communication as another learned skill. You must understand your receiver regardless of whether it is one person or a group of people. The age, experience, knowledge of language, interest, and background of your receiver is important. Make your message and delivery of it fit your receiver. Use words and examples that are clear and understandable to the receiver.

I remember working on a plan that was to be edited by the company's vice president. In my first draft I wrote, "If the elevator should fail do the following." The vice president changed it to read, "If the vertical transport should malfunction do the following." We argued several days over this change, but it remained as edited in the final version. Still, right before going to press the vice president called me in to his office and asked me if anyone would understand the term *vertical transport*. Before I could answer, he said, "The hell with them." Do not make this mistake. We communicate with others; we do not communicate to them. Use words that are simple, commonplace, and understandable.

You must listen to the receiver; this is FEEDBACK. Feedback is any information about your message, such as "I understand," or "You're wrong," or "What do you mean by that?" Feedback also can be nonverbal. A person who turns away from you while you are speaking gives you feedback about the reception of your message. Feedback gives you another chance to improve your communication so that understanding can occur.

Effective communication is not quick or easy. It takes time and practice. You may have to repeat a message several times before understanding occurs. Do not make the mistake of believing that just because you send a message understanding should take place. I remember going to dinner at a friend's house (the friend had arrived from Russia only six months before). Almost all the other dinner guests spoke Russian and spoke almost no English. Not speaking or understanding Russian myself, and wanting to know how this person felt about being in the United States and how life was in Russia, we started a conversation. I don't know if having a quart bottle of vodka for every two dinner guests helped or hindered the attempt but, after many attempts, good communication occurred. Yet it was not quick, nor was it easy. It was like giving birth—it was a struggle!

Effective communication is a struggle. To improve your communication you must practice. Practice sending messages to different types of receivers. Practice receiving and interpreting feedback. Practice listening to other senders.

A mistake made by some senders is to assume that if you ask, "Do you understand?" and the receiver answers, "Yes, the receiver really understands. Yet too often the receiver only thinks he understands but lacks real understanding. So the sender goes on his way thinking effective communication has occurred and a few days later wonders how his action plan became so confused.

Never ask, Do you understand? The question to ask is, What do you understand? Remember, confirm, confirm, and confirm that your message was not only received but UNDERSTOOD.

The best communicators—people like John F. Kennedy, Ronald Reagan, and Martin Luther King, Jr.—did not communicate in words; they communicated with pictures, emotions, and examples to send their message. These communicators understood that one picture is worth a thousand words. To communicate effectively it is easier to convey pictures than it is to convey words, language, and symbols. Think in terms of sending your messages by way of a picture highway filled with emotions and examples.

☐ LESSON #12: ACTIONS SPEAK LOUDER THAN WORDS

We all learned to communicate nonverbally before we learned to talk or write. A mother understands when her baby is hungry without the child speaking a word.

Actions really do speak louder than words. If a person sends two messages, one spoken and the other by his body language (nonverbal actions), and if the messages are inconsistent, the nonverbal message will have a greater priority with the receiver. Think about the last time you believed a used car salesman or a politician. Why? Because, based on your experience, their words often conflicted with their actions. They said one thing but did another.

A major lesson that I learned as a child growing up on the streets of Philadelphia: Don't believe what a person tells you; believe your eyes. I'll believe it when I see it. Words are easy but actions are difficult. Because actions are difficult, they always count.

☐ LESSON #13
PERFORMANCE

Performance is the sum of your actions, the good ones and the bad ones. Performance not only counts, but it is the only thing that *does* count. We judge others and we are judged by others based upon actions or performance.

Have you ever heard anyone say it's OKAY for a batter to strike out or for a football player to fumble the football? I wouldn't think so. Why? Because you expect certain actions, a certain performance from those players, and when you don't receive them, you feel cheated. When they do not perform, you are cheated.

MAKE YOUR PERFORMANCE COUNT. Improve those things you can improve. Continue challenging yourself. Be accountable to yourself for your actions and performance.

☐ LESSON #14: SYSTEMS

As an undergraduate student in college, I had to take a physical science; I chose biology. It was the study of biology, especially the study of the human body, which gave me a special appreciation for systems. The human body is nothing more than a collection of systems working together in perfect harmony. Your circulatory system, skeletal system, muscular system, neurologic system, digestive system, immune system, etc. make you the human system.

Working your way through life's highways requires a special appreciation for systems. No matter what you can think of, it belongs to a system, such as weather systems, highway systems, economic systems, political systems, religious systems, governmental systems, military systems, medical systems, and legal systems, just to mention a few.

To appreciate a system you must understand its parts and subparts. You must understand not only how all the parts fit together but also how they relate to each other. The human body is a perfect example. At first glance it seems that the human body is operating by itself, without aid from other systems. Yet a closer examination reveals that without air to breathe, without food to eat or water to drink, without sleep, the body as a system would not operate. We are dependent upon many systems for survival.

Understanding that often the actions of one system will affect the actions, behavior, and results of other systems. Before you attempt to change a system, understand the relationship and the special balance that exists between the systems. The changes you make within the system may affect other parts. Sometimes the change we think will help one system negatively affects another system. It is like a puzzle—you must first figure out if you have the right pieces, and then you must decide how the pieces will fit together.

LEARN ALL YOU CAN ABOUT SYSTEMS.
NEVER STOP LEARNING ABOUT THEM.

☐ LESSON #15 : LEARNING, EDUCATION, AND PRACTICE

Learning takes place throughout one's life. From the time you are born till the time you die, learning occurs. Learning can be a great, rewarding experience, or it can be an unpleasant task. You need to choose! Open your mind to the learning experience. Learn to experience different things. Read books, articles, and magazines. Since we never stop learning, we can never learn everything, but we can strive to learn as much as we can.

Learning should not be confused with education. Education is the formal process of learning select information. I've told people often that I received most of my learning growing up on the streets of Philadelphia. Yet I received my education and refinement at college and the university. I know many people who do not have a formal education but who are very learned people. Schools are a resource for learning, but they are not the only resource for learning. We place too much responsibility on teachers and school administrators for educating; they are only one out of a multitude of resources for learning.

If practice does not make perfect, it sure helps. To learn any skill—a language, to read or write, to throw a baseball, or drive a car—you MUST practice if you hope to gain that skill. Practice is the process of repeating skills and concepts until they become second nature, until you can do them blindfolded or in your sleep. No matter how much of an expert you are in any subject, you must always practice to gain a greater level of skill. This is why professional athletes who achieve greatness on the playing field still practice the basic and advanced skills.

MAKE AN INVESTMENT IN YOURSELF BY PRACTICING.

☐ LESSON #16: WHY?

ASKING QUESTIONS IS HOW WE LEARN. Yet we fear asking a question that may sound dumb, so we don't ask the question and we don't learn. Now that is dumb.

Try to overcome your fear of asking questions because true understanding can only result from asking, Why?

REMEMBER: THERE ARE NO DUMB QUESTIONS.
EVERY QUESTION NEEDS TO BE ASKED.

☐ LESSON #17: FEAR AND THE UNKNOWN

Fear is a natural body defense mechanism—it protects us. When we see fire, a dark cave or hear an unknown noise, we become afraid. Fear can make us think about the correct actions to take, whether to fight or run. Fear also can paralyze you to the point where you don't take any action or you take the wrong action (like not asking questions), which can be harmful to you.

OVERCOME YOUR FEARS BY EXPLORING THEM.

I am afraid of heights. I cannot climb a ladder without becoming afraid. Yet I have explored this fear and have successfully fought off the paralysis that results from it. Not only have I climbed ladders and traveled over 50,000 miles by airplane, but I have flown in a helicopter over the San Francisco Bay. This was what would have to be one of the most exciting rides I have ever taken, just for the fun of it and to explore my fear.

☐ LESSON #18: FALSE GODS

There are those who are not true heroes, idols, or gods but only appear to be. The false gods create an illusion of greatness so powerful that it makes you forget who you are, where you are, and, most importantly, those people who are dear to you. THERE WILL BE A TIME IN YOUR LIFE WHEN A FALSE GOD WILL TRY TO TAKE CONTROL OF YOUR WILL; YOU MUST RESIST.

This is a tale of two uncles. Both uncles were in my life from the beginning. Yet when I was five one uncle decided to leave Philadelphia without telling anyone where he was going. No one in my family heard from him until eleven years had passed. The other uncle shared a part of himself with me throughout those eleven years. One day, as if by magic, the missing uncle reappeared. To me, he was larger than life—someone from my past that I could not touch until now. But this uncle practiced the fine art of creating illusions through speech. I wanted to be with him day and night. His lure was so powerful and, I believed, so sincere. I cared about nothing, especially not the other uncle who cared about me for all those years.

A year passed and the uncle who quickly came back into my life just as quickly left it again. I did not see him again until I was twenty-eight years old, but this time I was not fooled. He decided not to see me again even though we lived in the same city. Many years passed, and I visited him in the hospital where he was dying. Even on his deathbed he tried to use his illusions to win me over.

False gods will come and they will go, and their attraction will be very strong. Still you must keep the balance between their attraction and those people who really care about you, or you risk losing forever those people who care.

☐ LESSON #19: ALL WE NEED IS LOVE

LOVE is the one thing we all search for from birth till death. Unlimited is our need for love. We can never realize ultimate pleasure or ultimate love, so we keep searching. Humans are social animals; as such we need and want social contact with other humans. We go through life seeking the approval and love of our family, peers, friends, teachers, etc.

To win friends, you have to give a little love although giving love may be more difficult than receiving it. I have never seen a person refuse a kind word, even when a person is angry; I've seen a kind word melt the hostility. Most of the successful people I know all have one thing in common—they make people feel good. Try it. Find something good to say about a person and watch the person's facial expressions, then watch the positive results.

☐ LESSON #20: IN SEARCH OF LOVE (Peer Pressure)

Because we are always searching for love, the love of one's peers can be both rewarding and very dangerous. In seeking approval of one's peers, I have seen people do some crazy things, such as take drugs, submit to sex, wear clothes that are not to their liking, and risk their life. The need for peer approval is so strong that it can capture your soul.

BEWARE OF PEER PRESSURE

Balance your need for peer love with your self-respect and self-worth. Think about the requests and commands of your peers. Do they put your life in jeopardy? Is a little love worth the risk?

☐ LESSON #21: ENVIRONMENT (A State of Mind)

There is controversy regarding the degree of importance environment plays in shaping a person's abilities, characteristics, and behavior. Some say environment is so important that it determines one's probability of success or failure. I am here to say, ENVIRONMENT IS A STATE OF MIND.

I know some wealthy people living in large, modern houses located in some of the best areas who are some of the most unhappy and maladjusted people on the planet. Yet I also know some very happy people who live in relatively humble settings.

I have never believed that one is a prisoner of one's environment. Some prisoners living in the hell of Nazi concentration camps during World War II survived the horror of the physical environment by somehow separating themselves from their nightmarish surroundings.

An environment is an experience that can add to one's total experiences. Some environments give a person an advantage, but the degree of the advantage is uncertain. I have been in an environment where there was nothing to eat but a mustard sandwich. I have also had cocktails at the White House with a United States president. Each environment provided different experiences and opportunities. Each experience was equally important to my development.

I do not buy the story that because someone lives in a poor environment it means their chances of success decreases. I have seen many poor people become very successful in spite of their environment, or maybe because of it.

Don't let your environment affect your success or failure. You control your own destiny. That is not to say that you may not have to work harder than someone else. Remember, environment is a state of mind; your physical environment is escapable.

As a child I would escape my physical environment by going to the movies. Inside the darkened theater, I could travel around the world, eat in the finest restaurants, and have a million adventures. I now choose not to escape my physical environment but rather to expand it. You can expand your environment by reading, watching television, going to a concert or a sporting event, etc.

    IMPROVE YOUR MIND AND YOU WILL IMPROVE YOUR
                PHYSICAL ENVIRONMENT.

☐ LESSON #22: THE 22 BILLION DOLLAR MOVE

The year was 1975. I was hired as a transportation planner for the Federal Reserve Bank of Philadelphia. My first assignment was the preparation and implementation of a plan to move twenty-two billion dollars in currency, securities, and coin from the old building to a newly constructed building. For someone who lacked transportation or planning experience this was a challenging and exciting project to work on—a project that taught me the importance and need to plan and test every aspect of an operation.

Because we were moving money, certain conditions and limitations were placed on the move by the U.S. Government. The movement of currency and securities could only take place on a Saturday between midnight and 8:00 A.M. It was felt that it would be easier to secure the route during this period when there was less traffic. Only one armored car could be loaded at a time, and only one armored car could be on the street at any given time to reduce the Bank's financial exposure. The exact date of the move would not be known until the Friday before the move, and once known all personnel involved in the move were sworn to secrecy.

These conditions made the move very difficult because we had only eight hours to complete the first phase (movement of currency and securities). Thus every aspect had to be timed with very little room left for error. Additionally, we contracted with an armored car carrier (Purolator). We were relying on their trucks, personnel, and management to do the job. You can control your own personnel's performance, but we were uncertain about controlling the performance of another company. This would be an unknown that would have to be known before the move.

The planning and testing took about one year to complete. We tested everything—the size and type of containers, types and performance of various armored trucks, the amount of time it took to load a truck, the amount of time to drive the move route, various safety and personnel scenarios.

We discovered many problems during the planning and testing period. This is just part of the list:

1. Some armored cars did not function as well as others and had to be replaced.
2. The wooden containers used to hold the currency and securities broke open during transport.
3. Power lifts on the armored cars drained their batteries. Additional batteries plus auto mechanics and a tow truck were needed for the move.
4. Communications did not function well.
5. Safety gear was needed by the personnel.

It was a Friday afternoon on a hot July day in the year 1976 when I was told that the move would begin at midnight. I attended a security briefing by the Bank's chief security officer. FBI reports were given, indicating that several known bank robbers were in our area, but these individuals were being watched. The security plan was unveiled. A force of Bank personnel, FBI, Secret Service, and local police department personnel would interact to protect the money and people involved in the move. Only one vehicle could move at any given time, and each vehicle would be protected by a front and rear Secret Service car. Sharpshooters, helicopters, and police personnel were placed along the move route. The plan even called for an anti-tank weapon in case a tank appeared. Also, the plan contained information on what to do if a family member were taken hostage. Additionally we were told that being outside near the move route after midnight without the proper identification would mean a night in jail. Proper identification meant your Bank photo identification card plus a special colored arm band. The security briefing ended, and for the first time I became keenly aware of a sense of mission, purpose, and an understanding of the special nature of this operation.

Between afternoon and midnight I had much work to do. Vehicles had to be inspected, vehicle identification markers had to be in place, and timetables had to be reviewed and revised. At the completion of these tasks everything was in place. My manager, Chuck Clayman, took me out to dinner (I owe Chuck a lot because he believed in me and he had the faith that I could be successful in completing my assignments). Walking back to the bank around

8:00 P.M. I asked him after all the planning and testing how sure he was that it would work; he answered that he was about 50 percent sure. Still I knew without all that work the percentage would have been a lot smaller.

The move was successful. All the money was successfully moved without incident. Execution was nearly perfect, and we finished one hour ahead of schedule.

LESSON #23
GOOD vs. EVIL

In each of us there is the capacity to do great good and great evil. History has examples of both. Moses, Jesus Christ, Martin Luther King, Jr., and Mother Teresa are some people who have done great good. Adolph Hitler, Joseph Stalin, and Saddam Hussien are some people who have done great evil. The historical landscape is also littered with mild-mannered and somewhat good people whom in times of fear, anger, or rage have killed someone or who have done some sort of evil. The Holocaust, the Vietnam War, and the U.S. Civil War all have examples of such horrors.

Understand that you have the capacity to do both good and evil and that in every situation YOU MUST CHOOSE between them. Though the above examples contain overwhelming numbers of horrors, there are many examples of people who during these difficult times chose to do good. Also be aware that you share space with those people who will choose to do great evil; you must try to protect yourself from harm.

☐ LESSON #24: THE WORLD IS A DANGEROUS PLACE

If history teaches us anything it is that the world is a very dangerous place. From the beginning war has been a way of living and dying, man verses man. The following is a brief list of wars fought: The U.S. Revolutionary War (1776), French Revolution (1792), Revolutions in France, Belgium, parts of Germany, Italy, Switzerland, and Poland, and the Spanish Civil War (1830), U.S. Civil War (1864), The Indian Wars, First World War (1914), Spanish Civil War (1936), Second World War (1939-45), Korean War (1951), Vietnam War (1963-75), Israel War of Independence and the Six Day War, and The Invasion of Lebanon. It is said that most, if not all, wars are fought because of some noble purpose. Yet I submit that most wars, if not all, are fought because of some economic purpose, such as land, natural resource, money, etc. The haves want to protect what they have and the have nots want to get what belongs to the haves. Because resources are limited, we probably will always face war scenarios. If the above disturbs you, take comfort that on any given day, in any given place in the world, people are murdered, injured, and killed in automobile, train, and plane accidents. YES, THE WORLD IS A VERY DANGEROUS PLACE, SO TRY TO PROTECT YOURSELF.

☐ LESSON #25: LIFE ROADS

If you understand anything by now, you should understand that life is NOT a straight highway. On the interstate highway of life it is a bumpy ride filled with intersections, crossroads, detours, and choices of opportunity.

Every time you travel a new road, you are exploring new possibilities, but you are also forsaking other possibilities that are on other roads. This is a fact of the road of life so don't worry about what you have given up or missed; be more concerned with what you have gained.

The Chinese character for crisis is the same as the character for opportunity. Within every crisis lies some new opportunity that can be found. On my office wall hang two statements: "One must pass through a little rain to walk through a rainbow," and "There is no substitute for hard work and dedication." If you keep these statements in mind, you can help yourself through any crisis.

Travel life's roads with challenge and eagerness. Never look back in regret, but, rather look forward to each beginning.

☐ LESSON #26: THE WORLD IS A STAGE

Remember that we are different people every minute of the day. At one time we can play the role of father, and at another time we can be a businessman, and at another time we can be a husband or a teacher or a child. Understand that no matter how well you think you know someone, you may not really know that person unless you have seen all their possible roles.

☐ LESSON #27: RISK REDUCTION

Every time we walk down the street or drive in a car down a highway, we are taking a RISK. The RISK is that another person, intentionally or unintentionally, will do harm to us. We take these risks because we believe that the chance of failure is small. Yet there are times when we take risks that are too great.

I love the card game Blackjack or Twenty-one because it reflects life and helps me to sharpen my skills as a risk taker. The objective of Blackjack is to take as many cards as possible without going over twenty-one. To make the game a little bit harder you have to play against the casino (House). If the dealer has a sixteen and you have a fourteen, though you did not go over twenty-one you lose because the House has a better hand. In Blackjack as in life you must make very quick decisions with very limited information. You must take certain calculated risks, and you DON'T WIN EVERY TIME YOU PLAY.

Risk-taking is a part of life, but you must learn to take calculated risks and avoid those risks where the probability of failure and the consequence of failing are both too great.

☐ LESSON #28: THE HAND IS QUICKER THAN THE EYE

I've spent a good deal of my life learning about magic. I really appreciate an excellent illusionist, and I have seen some really great ones perform. What makes a great illusion is that the magician skillfully blends trickery and reality. The illusion is making the audience believe that the impossible is possible.

Life is full of illusions and illusionists. BE CAREFUL NOT TO BE FOOLED BY SUCH PEOPLE. You must be able to separate FACT from FICTION. You must look at each situation and be able to see the mirrors that create an illusion.

☐ LESSON #29: THE POWER OF LAUGHTER

The ability to laugh, especially at ourselves, is one of the most powerful tools we have to combat depression, loneliness, illness, and feelings of hopelessness.

As a child I remember sitting in front of the television watching the Three Stooges, Our Gang, The Marx Brothers, and other wonderful comedies. These comedies made me feel better and gave me a new outlook on life. No matter how rough times were economically in our house, we could always laugh.

There are positive physical changes that take place in the body when you laugh. These changes will make you healthier and will clear your mind for more important tasks.

MAKE SURE YOU LAUGH OFTEN IN YOUR LIFE. THE POWER OF LAUGHTER WILL SET YOU FREE.

☐ LESSON #30: RELAXATION IS GOOD FOR THE MIND

I learned this lesson late in my life, but fortunately not too late. A strong and relaxed body makes for a stronger mind. You cannot be in mental shape if your body is out of shape. If you are tense and stress has the best of you, your thought process will be affected.

SO LEARN HOW TO RELAX.

EAT THE RIGHT FOODS.

TAKE OFF SOME POUNDS.

EXERCISE TO FEEL BETTER.

There is a time to work, and work hard, but there also needs to be a time to play and relax. So make that time any way you can by bowling, swimming, walking, biking, playing team sports, etc. RELAX AND HAVE FUN. ENJOY THE PROCESS OF CLEARING YOUR MIND.

☐ LESSON #31: PLAY THE CARDS THAT ARE DEALT

It is a useless effort and wasted time to complain or analyze why bad things happen, especially when they happen to you. Problems, obstacles, and crises occur in everyone's life. Stop complaining and look for the positive road, the road that leads you past the obstacle or out of the crisis. You'll be surprised at the tough things, both physical and mental, that you can do.

One of the toughest things I've had to do in my life was to, on the same day, attend the funeral of my Grandfather Sam in the morning and in the afternoon attend the wedding of my sister. On that day I was riding an emotional roller coaster, going from extreme sadness and depression to extreme joy. It was a day of both physical and mental challenge, an extraordinary twenty-four hours in which I learned that I could deal with tough problems. During that time I never asked, Why is this happening to me, probably because I didn't have time to ask the question. I just played the cards that were dealt to me the very best way I could.

LIFE IS LIKE A CARD GAME;
SOME HANDS ARE GOOD, SOME HANDS ARE BAD,
AND
YOU DON'T HAVE MUCH CONTROL OVER THE DEALER
OR
HOW THE CARDS COME YOUR WAY.
SO PLAY THE CARDS THAT ARE DEALT TO YOU
THE VERY BEST WAY YOU CAN.

☐ LESSON #32: REAL MEN

Real men are strong-minded, but they can consider all points of view. They take care of their family and family matters. They are emotional and can show their emotion to others.

☐ LESSON #33: REAL WOMEN

Real women are strong-minded, but they can consider all points of view. They take care of their family and family matters. They are emotional and can show their emotion to others.

☐ LESSON #34: CHANGE

Change occurs every micro-second of every day. Some changes will affect you positively; some changes will affect you negatively. Either way, change *will* occur, so don't fight it. The thing we hate about change is that what we are changing to is unfamiliar, and we do fear the unknown. You must fight this fear and look at the change as an opportunity to travel a new life road.

THERE WILL BE MANY CHANGES IN YOUR LIFE. SOME WILL BE TRAGIC AND SOME WILL BE JOYOUS, BUT YOU MUST DEAL WITH ALL THE CHANGES.

☐ LESSON #35: TIME IS NOW

Time is a limited resource that is running out. Time is precious and should not be wasted. Time is something we never really have enough of.

A person who lives 70 years has lived in time 840 months, or 25,550 days, or 613,000 hours, or 36,792,000 minutes, or 2,207,520,000 seconds.

Most people spend about 33 percent of their time in a resting or sleeping state. Another way to look at it is that we have about 67 percent of our time to do whatever we want to do. Since we do not know how much time we really have, do you want to waste the 67 percent of your unknown amount of time?

YOUR TIME IS NOW; DON'T WASTE IT!

☐ LESSON #36: INFORMATION, PLEASE

Information is knowledge, and knowledge is power. The one point I've learned in years of negotiating is the person with the best information has an edge, has strength, and has power.

We live in the age of information. At your disposal are computers with data banks of information; television that can provide facts, images, and information from any place in the world as events are happening; books; newspapers; radios; etc. Never in world history has information been more readily available and as quickly attainable as right now.

THE INFORMATION-GATHERING TOOLS ARE JUST THAT—
TOOLS TO BE USED.
YOU MUST LEARN HOW TO GATHER INFORMATION,
AND MORE IMPORTANTLY,
YOU MUST LEARN HOW TO USE THE INFORMATION WISELY.
LEARN HOW TO SEPARATE FACT FROM FICTION.
LEARN HOW TO THINK!

☐ LESSON #37: TENNIS, EVERYONE!

I never took a tennis lesson to learn how to play the game of tennis. I picked up a racket and began to hit the ball. Then I read everything I could about the game. Then I spent hours watching professionals and non-professionals play the game. In doing so I learned not only the rules, but I also gained a healthier appreciation of the sport. Then I practiced, practiced, and practiced until I became a proficient player (not a championship player but a very good competitive player). To this day I enjoy picking up a racket and playing the game.

If you want to do something, don't wait for the lessons, fancy clothes, expensive rackets—just go out there and do it. The rest will come later.

☐ LESSON #38: GREAT TALENT WILL FIND YOU; ALL YOU NEED TO DO IS RECOGNIZE IT

A talented manager must have the ability to find the very best talent for every position in the organization. Great talent will find you; all you need is the ability to recognize it. I pride myself on having this ability—being able to separate the skilled from the great from the very great.

When I was learning the game of tennis as a teenager, my friend Irv Alper and I decided to expand our horizons (you remember my lesson on changing your environment). We traveled by public transportation from the urban setting of South Philly to the country club setting of Chestnut Hill (I mean blueblood society), where the Philadelphia Cricket Club was gathered to watch the final match of the girls sixteen and under tennis championships. I can't remember if we were more interested in tennis or watching the girls in short dresses. We arrived at the tennis club about four hours before the start of the match so we had plenty of time to kill. We decided to meet and talk to the players. I remember spending time with a sixteen-year-old tennis player who lived in Florida. I took her picture, and she told me that she was playing in the final match that very afternoon. I wished her luck and took my seat for the match. That afternoon, watching her play was a thing of great beauty. It was as if the sky had opened up and a lightning bolt hit me. She was good, very good, and I just knew that this player was not average, not just very good—she was bound for GREATNESS. Chris Evert won that match and I congratulated her. Now you know the rest of my story.

I was attending the inaugural Ball for the Governor of Pennsylvania. At the end of the evening I noticed a young TV news reporter from Philadelphia, Jane Robelot. Jane was not a native of my hometown, but as a recent newcomer she was doing a fine job on TV and I wanted to meet her. My wife felt the same way, so we strolled over and introduced ourselves. The reception we got was as if we were old friends, and although it was late in the evening, her energy level was sky high. After exchanging information about ourselves, I asked if she would have a permanent news anchor job. She laughed and said, "I don't think so, not for a long time, anyhow." We said goodnight and parted. I turned to my wife and said, "She doesn't even know that she will have an anchor spot sooner than she thinks." I had never met Jane before that evening, and I had no inside information or influence with the TV station. I just sensed greatness from the person. About a month later I called Jane to congratulate her on getting a new position with the station—you guessed it—the permanent 6:00 P.M. news anchor.

The year was 1973. I went to the opening night of a new musical comedy that was making its Philadelphia tryout before hopefully moving on to Broadway. The show was "Grease," and it was billed as "The New 50's Musical Comedy Hit." The show was very funny, and I found the music very entertaining. I fell in love with the show. The next day some cast members were doing a publicity event at one of the local department stores. I attended the event and got to talk to the cast members. I remember thinking to myself that these people, although somewhat unknown to the public, were very talented actors and singers. I wished each cast member luck in making the show a hit when it got to New York City. The show was very successful, and some cast members went on to star on stage, screen and television: John Travolta, Marilu Henner, Jeff Conaway, and Michael Lembeck.

YOU WILL FIND TALENT AND GREATNESS IN THE MOST UNEXPECTED PLACES; ALL YOU HAVE TO DO IS RECOGNIZE IT.

☐ LESSON #39: THE END OF THE ROAD

The two signs that hang on my office wall:

>There is no substitute for hard work
>
>and
>
>dedication.

>One must pass through a little rain to stand under a rainbow.

I did not know how important or true those statements were until the end of the road came. I worked for Professional Paramedical Service (PPS) from 1983 until 1989. PPS provided transportation service (paratransit and limousine services). We had built one of the largest and best companies in the Philadelphia industry, with over 100 vehicles on the street every day supplying services all across the city. Yet when the end of the road came, it came quickly, and we were not prepared for the aftermath.

It was 1988; our largest revenue source, the Commonwealth of Pennsylvania, changed not only the method of payment but also the amount of payment to the point where the expense of providing service was greater than the revenue received for providing such service. Simultaneously the limousine business took a nosedive. It didn't take long to realize that the ship was sinking and sinking fast. Creditors were calling me every day for payments we could not make. Our bank was nervous because we had borrowed a large amount of money to stay afloat. Our bankers were not certain if the debt would be repaid. Employee moral was at its lowest point, tensions were running high, and tempers were even hotter than usual—not the picture of team harmony that existed only six months before the crisis. I found myself waking up in the middle of the night in a panic. I didn't know if I could pay our employees for that week or which creditor would be at my doorstep in the morning. The physical and mental stress was unbearable.

Yet we restructured the company, made settlements with our creditors, laid off employees (one of the most difficult tasks I had to do was to let people go, some of whom had worked with me for five years), constructed a new financing arrangement with the bank, and simultaneously we started a brand-new corporation, Procor, to provide ambulance service. So as one organization was dying, a new organization was being born. Today Procor is the leading private-for-profit ambulance company in Philadelphia. The success did not come overnight; it took three years of hard work and walking through some rain storms.

I learned many important lessons during this time, most of which confirmed my belief in myself. Even in the darkest hours when crisis and stress were extreme, I kept my wits and did the impossible. Having faith and the need to continue may be enough, and at times it may be all that you have to count on.

☐ LESSON #40: FAITH AND MIRACLES

July 4, 1982 was not only a celebration of the birth of our nation but was the celebration of the birth of my son and the realization that miracles can happen, if you have faith.

It was a joyous occasion, the birth of my second child. Mother and son were fine; we were calling friends and relatives with the good news, and we were celebrating the joy of a new life.

Only a few hours had elapsed between the time of this new life coming into the world and the time I went down to the hospital's nursery to look at him with my cousin Cheryl. The doctor came out and spoke the words that changed my life forever: "Your baby is very sick; he may not make it." How can a healthy baby in a matter of a few hours turn into a baby that was dying? I went back to my wife's room and told her that his life was in God's hands. I believed that my son would live if he was strong enough and if he had the desire to live. The next few days I did much crying and praying. Yet I never lost faith. It never seemed hopeless though I knew the same facts that the doctors had told us: a newborn with this type of illness does not usually recover.

It was early in the morning when I walked into the Intensive Care Nursery. Dr. Rock greeted me with, "I don't believe it. This baby should be dead, but instead he pulled out his chest tube. Do you know the strength that a newborn needs to do that?" Brian still had a long way to go before recovering, but at that moment I knew my faith had paid off—my son would recover.

Today the only scars remaining from that illness are two small ones on Brian's chest where the chest tubes were inserted. Yet the lessons about faith and miracles will never be forgotten.

> FAITH IS BELIEVING EVEN WHEN THE FACTS AND INFORMATION SUGGEST THAT YOU SHOULD NOT.
> NEVER LOSE FAITH. KEEP BELIEVING IN MIRACLES.
> MIRACLES DO OCCUR.
> I HAVE LIVING PROOF OF IT.

☐ LESSON #41: IT'S NOT WHERE YOU START THE RACE, IT'S WHERE YOU FINISH THAT COUNTS

If you become discouraged because it takes you longer to learn something or because you are not as strong or proficient as others, DON'T be discouraged. Remember there are horses that take the lead early and then lose it because they don't have what it takes to endure. It is better to start out slow and steady and win than to start out strong and fast and lose.

☐ LESSON #42: IT STARTS WITH THE CUSTOMER

One of my pet peeves is the lack of customer service provided by many service organizations. I get so mad when I find stores, restaurants, and other service industries treating the customer as though the organization is doing them a favor in providing service. We have succumbed to a system full of order-takers instead of salespeople.

It is very simple:

START WITH THE CUSTOMER, AND TREAT THE CUSTOMER AS A KING OR QUEEN.

Fortunately I learned this lesson early in life when I was working after school in a delicatessen. The owner of the store instructed me on the finer points of customer service. When I was stocking the shelves or cleaning up, he would tell me, "Remember, when a customer walks into this store, stop whatever you are doing and take care of the customer, and do it willingly, and do it with a smile because that customer pays your salary, the rent, and the light bill."

Many organizations talk a good game of customer service, but in reality they fall short of the customer service mark. Customer service is easy to talk about but it is much more difficult to get an organization to believe in doing everything it can for the customer. While on vacation, though, I found one organization so dedicated to customer service it made a believer out of me. I was always impressed with Disney World's friendliness, cleanliness, and fun atmosphere. Still, it took the following event to convince me it was an organization totally dedicated to providing excellent customer service. It was midnight; we were about to leave EPCOT and my daughter, age eight, wanted an ice cream cone. We stopped at a refreshment stand that was about to close and asked for a cold delight. The server scooped the ice cream on a cone and handed it to my daughter. The cone slipped from my daughter's hand onto the clean floor. Before I could open my mouth to speak, the server said, "I am sorry, sir. We are having many problems with those cones; here's another cone of ice cream—no charge.

It is generally easy to provide good customer service when everything is running smoothly, but the real mark of a service-conscious organization is can they do it always, even at midnight when the tired staff wants to go home.

If you are ever in the position of serving customers, remember this story, and don't just talk about customer service—PROVIDE IT and DO IT.

☐ LESSON #43: DEALING WITH BULLIES

Webster's Ninth New Collegiate Dictionary defines the word *bully* as "one habitually cruel to others weaker than himself."

THE ONLY WAY TO DEAL WITH A BULLY IS TO STAND UP TO HIM. SHOW THE BULLY THAT YOU ARE NOT WEAK.

When I was a young boy, my family moved into a new house. It was located on a street frequented by several bullies; I had to fight my way to and from school each day. These bullies had nothing better to do than to use me for a human punching bag, until one day I got angry because one of the weaker bullies had cursed my mother. I jumped on top of him and wrestled him to the ground. My hands were locked around his neck, squeezing and cutting off his air supply. It took my mother and two other people to pull me off of him. I almost killed him, but that was the last day that I had any problems with those bullies.

☐ LESSON #44: ECONOMIC REALITY

You don't need an MBA to understand economic reality. A quick economics lesson:

WANTS AND NEEDS ARE UNLIMITED. RESOURCES TO SATISFY THOSE WANTS AND NEEDS ARE LIMITED AND SCARCE.

With so many people in the world vying for the same resources, some people will have many and some people will have few. The people who have few will try to improve their ECONOMIC REALITY.

☐ LESSON #45: SEX—A HUMAN ACTIVITY

Hormones within the human body control the sex drive. At times this drive is so strong that it makes people behave in ways in which they normally would not. Marketers understand the power of the need for sex and use it to sell everything from toothpaste to cars.

I learned about sex the only way I could during adolescence—by talking to my friends. The amount of misinformation was incredible. In graduate school I took an excellent human sexuality course taught by a senior citizen. There were three males and fifteen females in the class, which made the questions not only interesting but at times somewhat embarrassing. Yet I did learn some important life lessons:

SEX IS AN IMPORTANT PART OF LIFE THAT CAN BE DISCUSSED, STUDIED, AND LEARNED.

THE PEOPLE INVOLVED CAN MAKE SEX A THING OF BEAUTY OR SOMETHING THAT IS DIRTY AND EVIL.

THINK ABOUT THE CONSEQUENCES THAT ARE CAUSED BY YOUR ACTIONS.

☐ LESSON #46: HATE

I have looked into the eyes of hate, facing it straight on, and it is ugly. Do not confuse hate with anger. It is all right to be angry with someone because of a problem that needs to be resolved, but hate is more than anger. Hate is not liking someone because of their religion, color, nationality, or because they are unlike you.

I understand HATE and the results of it. During high school, I saw enough hate to last me a lifetime. I saw race riots, fire bombings, students with slashed faces and gunshot wounds. On one day during a riot I was thrown down a flight of stairs by a group of black students. They did not know me, and their only reason for hating me was my skin color. A few days later a black classmate and friend told me he had seen the incident on the stairs but could not and would not do anything to stop it. At that moment I really understood HATE.

During my life I have been called "Jew Boy" more times than I care to count. I have been denied access in various situations because of my religious beliefs. One day during my Army stay I worked in the kitchen for a day. There I came in contact with a sergeant from the deep south who had never met a Jew. Upon learning that I was Jewish he called me over and said, "Hey, Jew Boy, are you really a Jew? I never seen a Jew before." Where's your horns, Jew boy?" Now, we are not talking about the 1940's or 1950's here; this happen in 1971, many years after the passage of the Civil Rights Act in the United States Army. Well, I got over that incident quickly, but I will never forget the face of HATE.

Now I don't want to lead you to believe that I don't hate because I do. I hate the following:

1. Ignorance
2. Poverty
3. The under-educated
4. Disease
5. Crime

☐ LESSON #47: YOUR SIDE OF THE LINE

There are at least two sides to every story. Your position about most things in life will depend upon WHAT SIDE OF THE LINE YOU'RE ON. In any argument the two sides will advance those facts which will enhance their own position. Poor people believe that the government does not do enough for them, and rich people believe that the government does too much. Yet if that same rich person becomes poor, he now is on the opposite side of the line and probably will change his position about poor people and the government.

KNOW WHAT SIDE OF THE LINE YOU'RE ON,

and

WHEN DEALING WITH OTHERS, KNOW WHAT SIDE OF THE LINE THEY'RE ON.

☐ LESSON #48: HYPOCRISY

Webster's Dictionary defines *hypocrisy* as "stimulation or pretense of goodness; feigning to be what one is not; insincerity."

Understand that life is full of hypocrisy, whether it is in government, family, religion, education, etc. Regardless of whether hypocrisy is within institutions or within individual members of society you must learn to look for it. Examine it, understand it, and act according to your beliefs and desires.

MAKE SURE YOUR ACTIONS ARE FREE FROM HYPOCRISY.

☐ LESSON #49: MAKE YOUR WORD YOUR BOND

We have become a society of lawyers and people who are ready to sue over the most minor situations, most of which occur because people give their word to do or not to do something and then they break that promise.

In business as well as in life, the most successful people all have one characteristic in common: they keep their promises.

DON'T MAKE A PROMISE YOU CAN'T KEEP.

KEEP PROMISES THAT YOU MAKE.

MAKE YOUR WORD YOUR BOND.

☐ LESSON #50: HEART

Having heart is like having an extra ingredient. It is having the extra drive, determination, and guts to go it alone, to fight against the odds. I have seen professional athletes with fewer skills than others overcome the odds and become winners because they had HEART. I have seen one man stand-off a crowd of fifty angry people with his only weapon being HEART. In 1980 I saw the USA hockey team beat probably a much better Russian hockey team to win the gold medal in the Olympics because they had much HEART. I have seen boxers with plenty of skill and talent become losers because they did not have HEART.

There is much to be said about having skill and talent, but never forget that extra ingredient: HEART!

☐ LESSON #51: LESS IS MORE

A professor taught me the concept and value of simplicity, the KISS concept: "Keep it Simple, Stupid." In a world full of complexity there is something to be said for brevity and keeping things simple.

WHENEVER POSSIBLE MAKE IT CLEAR
AND KEEP IT SIMPLE.

☐ LESSON #52: EXPERIENCE vs. YOUTH

The other day I was watching Jimmy Connors playing his heart out in the U.S. Open Tennis tournament. Here was a thirty-nine-year-old man playing against some of the best players in the world, many of whom much younger than he. An equally exciting battle between experience and youth that I remember watching was a professional boxing match where a forty-two-year-old former heavyweight champion was going against an opponent almost half his age. Very quickly the forty-two-year overweight boxer eliminated the younger challenger.

There is something to be said for youth, with its stamina and excitement. Yet there is also something to be said about the experience and wisdom that comes with age.

I remember the first day on the job at the Federal Reserve Bank. I had youth and not much more. I was introduced to a man who managed the coin operation for about twenty-five years. Over coffee he told me things about the Bank and its operations that I could not have learned from reading any book. He was a wealth of information and insight.

In our society it is easier to accept youth as a beginning than to recognize that youth lacks the experience that is gained through the years. We tend to ignore those who are old as having outdated ideas and thoughts when it is those very ideas, thoughts, and deeds that will be of value to us. Learn from the wisdom of those who have walked the path before you.

IF YOUR LIFE DEPENDED ON ANOTHER PERSON'S ACTIONS, WOULD YOU WANT THAT PERSON TO BE YOUNG OR EXPERIENCED?

☐ LESSON #53: A HANDICAP

I met an interesting woman at a dinner party who told me she was handicapped and proud of it! She did not consider herself abnormal, even if other people around her did. She had won five gold medals in the World Special Olympic Games held in England during the summer and was very proud of that fact.

This meeting reminded me of my grandfather, Sam Schwartz (Pop), and a lesson I learned early in life. In his late forties my grandfather suffered a stroke that paralyzed one side of his body and slurred his speech. I'll always remember my grandfather walking with a cane, but I never thought of him as handicapped or disabled because in his mind he was not. This man would travel from one end of the city to the other on public transportation (before access for the physically disabled became popular). If you tried to help him he would tell you to stop and go away. He was going to do it himself, going to do it his way. If you would look up the word *determination* in the dictionary, you would see a picture of my grandfather. That is how I will always remember him—as a man full of determination, willpower, and pride.

My grandfather taught me many lessons, but this is the most important lesson:

YOU MAY HAVE A PHYSICAL DISABILITY BUT YOU ARE NOT DISABLED; IF YOU ARE IT IS ONLY IN YOUR MIND.

☐ LESSON #54: DO YOU FEEL LUCKY TODAY?

I've played the games of chance at the casinos in Las Vegas and Atlantic City, where I gained a fair understanding of good and bad luck. As with any game of chace, including the game of life, being in the right place at the right time contributes just as much to winning as does skill. In any game of chance the odds are with the house (the casino). Over a period, over long term, the house will be the winner. If you play a game of chance often, you have a very good chance of losing. Still, the house will lose at times. That is the major reason people bet money on games of chance—they just might win and win BIG, if they're lucky.

At the age of fourteen I associated with men who were gamblers and bookmakers (managers of illegal games of chance). Most of these men would bet on anything—cards, professional sports, horse racing, or which old lady would make it across the street without getting hit by a car. I would walk into a room and someone would say, "Hey, kid, root for this team, and if they win I'll give you twenty bucks." Gamblers are very interested in luck, especially good luck, and the thinking is that maybe, just maybe, having more people praying for your team will bring you better fortune.

Some people are luckier than others. They seem to get all the right breaks, they are in the right games at the right time, etc.

THE MORE YOU PLAY THE GAME, THE MORE CHANCES YOU HAVE TO WIN OR LOSE.
DON'T UNDERESTIMATE THE ROLE OF LUCK, GOOD OR BAD, IN YOUR LIFE.

☐ LESSON #55: WHEN TWO WORLDS COLLIDE

Wally Loeb was my mentor, friend, and someone who would help guide my life from the time I was eight years old up through adulthood. Wally taught me many lessons and made many contributions to my growth and development. Early in our relationship he showed me that there were two worlds: my world of poverty and worry, and his world of wealth and ease.

The first time I met Wally's parents, he took me to their house for dinner. It was like a scene right out of a Hollywood movie; I thought I'd died and gone to heaven. The house was huge, with a large front lawn, rose gardens, and a tennis court. Inside the house were many bedrooms, each with its own bathroom, and a large dining room where we were served dinner by some very good domestic helpers. As a kid who was growing up in a row house with only one bathroom, I was star-struck. I was in awe that some people really lived like this. After all, I had only seen this lifestyle in the movies.

That experience more than any other gave me a vision of hope and an avenue of possibilities. It showed me that there were many worlds, including mine. I could become a part of any world at anytime.

WHEN TWO WORLDS COLLIDE, ANYTHING IS POSSIBLE.

☐ LESSON #56: THE CLASSLESS SOCIETY

    I grew up around people who used four-letter words as adjectives. You know the kind of words I mean—profanity. I think they used these words to make people believe that they were tough and should be feared (at least that is why I used them). Yet I finally learned that most of the world does not use these words. Using them will not make you look tough but will make you look stupid and uneducated.

    Sometimes I will see educated, professional people (corporate presidents, government people, teachers, doctors, lawyers, etc.) using profanity for the same reason I used it as a kid, and it turns me off. I think to myself, why are they using those words? Are they trying to make me believe that they are part of the classless society? Guess what—they are succeeding.

IF YOU WANT TO MAKE AN IMPRESSION BY USING PROFANITY, YOU WILL, BUT IT MIGHT NOT BE THE IMPRESSION THAT YOU WANT TO MAKE.

☐ LESSON #57: IMAGINATION AND DREAMS

Every new product, invention, movie, building, business, etc. starts with an idea or a dream in someone's mind. To build great things, you must first have the ability to imagine and dream great things. The writer H.G. Wells imagined putting a man on the moon years before it happened. We all have some ability to dream and use our imagination. As children we use our imagination to play games, role play, and journey through undiscovered new worlds. Yet as we grow older some of us limit the use of our imagination, and as with any skill if you don't use it you will lose it.

BUILD YOUR IMAGINATION AND DREAMING ABILITY BY THINKING OF ENDLESS POSSIBILITIES WITHOUT LIMITATIONS OR OBSTACLES.

KEEP ASKING THE QUESTION, WHAT IF?

☐ LESSON #58: SOLVE THE PROBLEM

As a manager, the major characteristic that distinguishes me from non-managers is my ability to make decisions and solve problems (which I am good at). Solving problems is how I earn my paycheck. Yet, more importantly having the ability to see small problems and to solve them before they grow into bigger ones makes me a really great manager. You can be sure of one thing about problems—they don't go away without help. If you leave a small problem alone, it will grow bigger and bigger until it becomes a crisis.

BECOME PROFICIENT IN RECOGNIZING PROBLEMS,

AND

TAKE THE REQUIRED ACTIONS

TO SOLVE THE PROBLEMS.

THERE ISN'T ANY PROBLEM THAT CAN'T BE SOLVED.

☐ LESSON #59: A LITTLE BIT OF KNOWLEDGE

During my senior year in high school, I sat in front of Lois Miller. I would turn to her before a test and say, "Lois, hit me with a little bit of knowledge." A little knowledge is all right and may help you pass a few tests. Yet for real understanding of a subject you must have more than just a little bit of knowledge. You must know the material like you know your name. Think about it: Would you like to be treated by a doctor who only has a little bit of medical knowledge or represented by a lawyer who only has a little knowledge of the law? I think not!

THERE IS NOTHING MORE DANGEROUS THAN A PERSON WHO HAS A LITTLE BIT OF KNOWLEDGE
EXCEPT
A PERSON WHO BELIEVES HE HAS MORE.

☐ LESSON #60: THE MEANING OF THE WORD SALE AND OTHER ECONOMIC CONCEPTS

While working for a large department store in Philadelphia, I realized the meaning of the word *sale*. Before this time I believed, like many other people, that the word *sale* meant bargain, savings, cheaper prices, etc., yet that is not necessarily true. What the word *sale* means is to sell a product or service. At the department store we had sales every day of the week: White Sales, Holiday Sales, Founders Day Sales, etc. People flocked to the store with the idea that they would save money, but many of the products that were on sale lacked a price reduction. This is not to imply that if you are a careful shopper you will not save money on some products, because you will, but you will not save money on all products that are ON SALE.

The phrase, "Going Out for Business" has trapped more people into believing that a store was selling merchandise at reduced prices because some people read those words as "Going Out of Business," which means a store is closing and must sell its merchandise. What the words "Going Out for Business" mean is nothing more than a store has some products to sell.

The words *reduced* or *reduction* have an impact on some people. If I tell you that a price is reduced by 40 percent, you might believe that was very good. Yet, reduced from what price: retail price, wholesale price, cost? Maybe the original price was 100 percent more than what other retailers charge. The fact is you just don't know.

DON'T PAY RETAIL PRICES FOR A PRODUCT OR A SERVICE
IF YOU CAN BUY IT FOR WHOLESALE PRICES;
AND
DON'T PAY FOR A PRODUCT OR A SERVICE
THAT YOU CAN GET FREE.
DON'T BE FOOLED BY SOME ECONOMIC WORDS.
GET THE FACTS
AND
LET THE BUYER BEWARE.

☐ LESSON #61: STICK TO THE BASICS

Whenever you feel your performance slipping, go back to the basics, back to the fundamental concepts you learned as a beginner. In doing so you will sharpen your skills and bring your performance back to a higher level. Professional athletes understand this concept because no matter how great an athlete is, he will always go back to practice and review the fundamentals of the sport. In reviewing employee performance I have found that many employees whose performance declines lose their edge because they take their eyes off the ball; they lose sight of the basic concepts, policies, and procedures.

KEEP YOUR EYES ON THE BALL,
AND
DON'T FORGET THE BASICS.

☐ LESSON #62: COMMON KNOWLEDGE, OR JUST THE FACTS, PLEASE

We will come to depend on and use common knowledge in our daily lives. Common knowledge is that knowledge which is compiled from part fact, part fiction, rumor, opinion, and misunderstanding. It is much easier to take and use common knowledge than to search for facts. Facts are those things that can be substantiated, such as dates of events, statistics, times related to occurrences, and weather conditions. Facts are objective where opinions are subjective. Common knowledge contains some facts but mostly opinions. There was a television show, Dragnet," in which the main character, Sergeant Friday, would always say, "Just the facts." To solve a crime or present a legal question to a jury or judge one must deal with the facts or evidence of a case. So it is true that one must try to get the facts when solving a problem, making a decision, buying a product or a service, choosing a course of action, or studying a subject.

MAKE SURE YOU CAN DETERMINE FACT FROM OPINION.

MAKE SURE YOU GET THE RELEVANT AND
THE TRUE FACTS.

☐ LESSON #63: GO FOR IT!

Be assertive, know what you want, and go for it. If you wait around for someone to give you charity or offer you a reward, you will probably be waiting for a long time. Don't wait; ask for it. If the answer is no, then ask again. You have nothing to lose by asking and everything to gain.

IF YOU DON'T ASK FOR IT, YOU'LL HAVE ZERO CHANCE OF GETTING IT.

☐ LESSON #64: IDEAS

The more ideas one has, the greater the likelihood of having a really great idea. Ideas are the thoughts one develops in their mind. Thus the more you practice thinking, the more ideas you will have. Brainstorming is the process of getting several people together to generate ideas. It's like a chain reaction—one person has an idea that leads to another person thinking about something, which generates another idea, and so on and so on.

KEEP THINKING

AND

COME UP WITH SOME GREAT IDEAS.

☐ LESSON #65: THE TEAM

It's great experience to watch individual musicians play in a band where the music sounds like one instrument. What an experience it is to see a championship sports team play the game as one unit. The most important lesson I learned in the Army was that the team is greater than any individual on the team. As a team member you must strive for excellence, and everyone on the team MUST help each other, especially those who are weaker, in times of crisis.

Networking is the art of establishing relationships with other people and seeking the advice of those with special knowledge.

MAKE YOU SPECIAL EXCELLENCE PART OF THE TEAM;
STRONG INDIVIDUALS MAKE A STRONG TEAM.
ANY INDIVIDUAL CAN ACHIEVE A LOT MORE WITH THE HELP OF OTHERS.
SEEK OUT PEOPLE AND ASK FOR THEIR HELP,
AND
WHEN ASKED GIVE HELP IN RETURN.

☐ LESSON #66: WINDOW OF OPPORTUNITY

Think of OPPORTUNITY as a window that opens briefly, allowing you to take hold of the chance. Yet if you don't take hold the window will close, shutting you off from the occasion. Successful people recognize or create opportunities. Also, they don't hesitate, they don't wait for the window to close; instead, they grab hold of an opportunity before the window shuts, claiming all its rewards. Some people can't recognize an opportunity when it is in front of them. They hesitate, taking their time to decide until it is too late and the window closes. Then you hear should have, could have, and would have. Remember, all the should haves and could haves won't pay the rent.

RECOGNIZE THOSE WINDOWS OF OPPORTUNITY.

DON'T HESITATE;

SEIZE THE OPPORTUNITY, MAKING IT YOURS.

☐ LESSON #67: ONE LOOK BACKWARDS, TWO STEPS FORWARD

Taking one look backwards will help you to move two steps forward. Looking at the past and reviewing your successes, failures, and places traveled will help to put the present and your future into perspective.

I recently had lunch with a friend that I had not seen in eighteen years. We reminisced and talked about our present lives. We both wondered what it would be like if we had taken different life roads. Yet we both knew that as a result of the roads we had traveled and the experiences we had gathered, we developed into the people that we are today. That one look backwards gave me a new perspective for the future. It helped me to appreciate where I have been and where I want to go; it helped me to move two steps forward.

> LOOK BACKWARDS TO SEE THE PRESENT
> MORE CLEARLY.

☐ LESSON #68: CONTINUATION

We, as individuals, are never complete, never finished; instead, we are always in the process of becoming.

Remember during the dark times in your life that any moment in time is not a conclusion but rather a continuation.

CONTINUE THE PROCESS OF BECOMING.

☐ LESSON #69: ZEST FOR LIFE

I recently interviewed two candidates for the same job. One woman had very little enthusiasm and it seemed like she was not very interested in getting the job; she was only going through the motions. The other woman had a high energy level and was very enthusiastic about the prospect of working for our company. Both job candidates had good qualifications for the job. Which woman do you think I hired?

If you just go through the motions, don't expect other people to get excited about you or your plans.

Create a high energy level in yourself and let your energy level explode. Let your enthusiasm shine. If you are not enthusiastic about doing something, you are probably doing the wrong thing. Find something else to do.

Having great qualifications is important, but if you are just going through the motions you will not succeed. You need to have a real zest for life, a real zest for the goal, a real zest for the job, etc.

☐ LESSON #70: RIDE THE ELEPHANT

It happened at the New Jersey State Fair. My seven year-old daughter wanted me to ride the elephant, a live and very big elephant. So I did; I overcame my fear of heights, and although all the color drained from my face, I rode the elephant. The feeling of accomplishment was great—doing something I had not done before, something new and exciting. After riding the elephant nothing else quite compares.

Whenever a new challenge presents itself, I think of my ride on the elephant and I take the challenge.

> TRY NEW AND EXCITING THINGS.
> CHALLENGE YOURSELF
> RIDE THE ELEPHANT.

☐ LESSON #71: DEATH

All living things eventually die—they end. It is nature's way of making room for the new and different. Death is a way of continuing life. You will find evidence of this by looking at the obituary page of any newspaper; on any day it is full of people who have recently died. On one Sunday I looked at the obituary page of the *Philadelphia Inquirer* and counted 110 people who died.

I have some experience with death because my father died in 1956, when I was five years old, leaving a painful void in my life which will never be filled. Death is painful for the living. Yet you must work through the pain and continue with the journey of life.

> REMEMBER THE DEAD
> AND
> KEEP THEIR EXPERIENCE AND SPIRIT ALIVE IN YOU
> THROUGHOUT YOUR LIFE.

LIFE

by Stephanie Schwartz

Gazing up at the clouds on a beautiful summer morning,
The cool, fresh breeze that gives movement to the trees
Driving to the beach with the hood down,
letting nature's beauty shine in.
But then finding yourself fighting through the traffic.
Now your mood has changed,
but once you take a whiff of the sea air you feel better.
Then you must find a space where you belong,
once you've found that place you must build your sandcastle.
If it falls down you have to build it up again,
this time making sure you have a stronger platform.
After you've built a strong sandcastle it's time to have fun.
You can go surfing, but even if you wipe out,
you have to get up and try again.
At last lying on the beach
and looking back on all that you've accomplished.
And then heading back home.
This to me is life.